little Miss Busy

by Roger Hargreaves

Little Miss Busy loved nothing more than to be hard at work, keeping herself busy.

As busy as a bee.

In fact, as busy as a hive of bees.

Every day she would get up at three o'clock in the morning.

Then, Little Miss Busy
would read a chapter from her favourite book.

It was called:
"Work is good for you".

And then she would get down to the housework.

She would begin by tidying up,
and then sweeping,
and dusting,
and scrubbing,
and polishing,
until everything was spotless.

She would clean her house from top to bottom
and then from bottom to top, just to make sure.

She even dusted the bread and polished the butter.

She wasn't happy unless she was busy working.

And she didn't rest all day long, not for a minute,
not even for a second.

From three o'clock in the morning
until after midnight.

That was until last Monday.

Little Miss Busy wasn't up at three o'clock.

She wasn't up by six o'clock.

She wasn't even out of bed by nine o'clock.

She was ill.

"Oh, calamity!" she cried.

"I won't be able to do any work!"

She telephoned Doctor Make-you-well.

Five minutes later he was at her bedside.

He asked her to put out her tongue.

He examined her throat.

And he looked at her hands and feet.

"What you need is rest, a lot of rest,"
he said, with a broad smile.

"A lot of rest," repeated Little Miss Busy to herself.

"Oh, calamity!"

There was a loud THUMP!

Which was the sound of Little Miss Busy
falling over backwards,
on to the bed,
luckily for her.

On Tuesday, Mr Strong
called to see Little Miss Busy.

He brought her 72 eggs.

Go on, count them.

"There is nothing like eggs
for giving you strength," said Mr Strong.

By the seventy-second egg,
Little Miss Busy was feeling much better.

That was, until Mr Strong said,
"Now you must rest to get your strength up."

There was a loud THUMP!

Which was the sound of Little Miss Busy
falling over backwards,
on to the bed,
luckily for her.

On Wednesday, Mr Greedy
came to visit.

He brought an enormous bowl of food.

"I always find that eating a big meal
makes me feel better," said Mr Greedy.

Little Miss Busy ate the lot.

She felt better than ever.

That was until Mr Greedy said,
"Now you must rest to let your stomach settle."

There was a loud THUMP!

And you know what that was, don't you?

That's right!

Little Miss Busy had fallen over backwards.

On Thursday, Mr Nonsense
popped in to see Little Miss Busy.

He brought her...an umbrella!

"Hello," he said.
"I hear you're feeling well. You don't need a rest..."

Little Miss Busy jumped for joy, right out of bed.
"...you need a holiday!" finished Mr Nonsense.

There was a loud THUMP!
That's right.
"There you look better already," said Mr Nonsense,
and left...

...by the open window.

Little Miss Busy picked herself up.

A small smile formed on her face.

Something Mr Nonsense had said
had actually made sense.

She had never thought of going on holiday before.

The more she thought about it the happier she felt.

She thought of all the fun things she could do.

There was the planning and organising,
there was all the shopping she would have to do,
there was the packing,
and she would have to learn the language,
and read lots of books about the place she was going to.

What a lot of work!

Little Miss Busy smiled happily.

The following Thursday, she was awake at three o'clock in the morning.

Everything was ready.

Little Miss Busy had had one of the busiest weeks of her life.

Which is saying something!

She had only one thing left to do.

And that was...

...to learn how to twiddle her thumbs!

3 Great Offers for MR.MEN Fans!

1 New Mr. Men or Little Miss Library Bus Presentation Cases

A brand new stronger, roomier school bus library box, with sturdy carrying handle and stay-closed fasteners.
The full colour, wipe-clean boxes make a great home for your full collection.
They're just £5.99 inc P&P and free bookmark!

☐ MR. MEN   ☐ LITTLE MISS (please tick and order overleaf)

2 Door Hangers and Posters

In every Mr. Men and Little Miss book like this one, you will find a special token. Collect 6 tokens and we will send you a brilliant Mr. Men or Little Miss poster and a Mr. Men or Little Miss double sided full colour bedroom door hanger of your choice. Simply tick your choice in the list and tape a 50p coin for your two items to this page.

PLEASE STICK YOUR 50P COIN HERE

Door Hangers (please tick)
☐ Mr. Nosey & Mr. Muddle
☐ Mr. Slow & Mr. Busy
☐ Mr. Messy & Mr. Quiet
☐ Mr. Perfect & Mr. Forgetful
☐ Little Miss Fun & Little Miss Late
☐ Little Miss Helpful & Little Miss Tidy
☐ Little Miss Busy & Little Miss Brainy
☐ Little Miss Star & Little Miss Fun

Posters (please tick)
☐ MR.MEN
☐ LITTLE MISS

en Beautiful Fridge Magnets – £2.00! any 2 for inc.P&P

very special collector's items!
ick your first and second* choices from the list below
2 characters!

		2nd Choice	
Mr. ppy	☐ Mr. Daydream	☐ Mr. Happy	☐ Mr. Daydream
Mr. Lazy	☑ Mr. Tickle	☐ Mr. Lazy	☑ Mr. Tickle
Mr. Topsy-Turvy	☐ Mr. Greedy	☐ Mr. Topsy-Turvy	☐ Mr. Greedy
☐ Mr. Bounce	☐ Mr. Funny	☑ Mr. Bounce	☐ Mr. Funny
☐ Mr. Bump	☑ Little Miss Giggles	☐ Mr. Bump	☑ Little Miss Giggles
☐ Mr. Small	☑ Little Miss Splendid	☑ Mr. Small	☑ Little Miss Splendid
☑ Mr. Snow	☑ Little Miss Naughty	☑ Mr. Snow	☑ Little Miss Naughty
☐ Mr. Wrong	☑ Little Miss Sunshine	☐ Mr. Wrong	☑ Little Miss Sunshine

*Only in case your first choice is out of stock.

TO BE COMPLETED BY AN ADULT

**To apply for any of these great offers, ask an adult to complete the coupon below and send it with
the appropriate payment and tokens, if needed, to MR. MEN CLASSIC OFFER, PO BOX 715, HORSHAM RH12 5WG**

☐ Please send _____ Mr. Men Library case(s) and/or _____ Little Miss Library case(s) at £5.99 each inc P&P

☐ Please send a poster and door hanger as selected overleaf. I enclose six tokens plus a 50p coin for P&P

☐ Please send me _____ pair(s) of Mr. Men/Little Miss fridge magnets, as selected above at £2.00 inc P&P

Fan's Name _____

Address _____

_____ **Postcode** _____

Date of Birth _____

Name of Parent/Guardian _____

Total amount enclosed £ _____

☐ **I enclose a cheque/postal order payable to Egmont Books Limited**

☐ **Please charge my MasterCard/Visa/Amex/Switch or Delta account** (delete as appropriate)

Card Number

Expiry date ___ / ___   **Signature** _____

Please allow 28 days for delivery. Offer is only available while stocks last. We reserve the right to change the terms
of this offer at any time and we offer a 14 day money back guarantee. This does not affect your statutory rights.
Data Protection Act: If you do not wish to receive other similar offers from us or companies we recommend, please
tick this box ☐. Offers apply to UK only.

MR.MEN   LITTLE MISS
Mr. Men and Little Miss™ & ©Mrs. Roger Hargreaves